ANIMALS
OF MY OWN KIND

Animals

of My Own Kind

NEW AND SELECTED POEMS

Harry Thurston

SIGNAL EDITIONS IS AN IMPRINT OF VÉHICULE PRESS

Published with the generous assistance of The Canada Council for the
Arts and the Book Publishing Industry Development Program of the
Department of Canadian Heritage.

SIGNAL EDITIONS EDITOR: CARMINE STARNINO

Cover design: David Drummond
Photo of author: Catherine Thurston
Set in Filosofia and Minion by Simon Garamond
Printed by Marquis Book Printing Inc.

LIBRARY AND ARCHIVES CANADA CATALOGUING IN PUBLICATION

Thurston, Harry, 1950-
Animals of my own kind / Harry Thurston.

Poems.
ISBN 978-1-55065-258-1

I. Title.

PS8589.H88A75 2009   C811'.54   C2009-903485-9

Published by Véhicule Press, Montréal, Québec, Canada
www.vehiculepress.com

Distribution in Canada by LitDistCo
orders@litdistco.ca
Distributed in the U.S. by Independent Publishers Group
www.ipgbook.com

Printed in Canada on 100% recycled paper.

for Catherine

Contents

NEW POEMS

Acknowledgments

I want to thank family and friends for the support they have provided over many years, especially Catherine Thurston, Meaghan Thurston, Greg Cook, Allan Cooper, Thaddeus Holownia, and Andrew Steeves. Also, I wish to thank the editor of this book, Carmine Starnino, for his interest in my work and his careful selection and editing of it.

I am grateful to the Nova Scotia Department of Tourism, Recreation and Culture for a Creator's Grant that allowed time to work on this collection. Also, thanks to the owners of Elizabeth Bishop House for the privilege of spending time there while I worked on new poems.

I also want to thank the editors of the following magazines and anthologies where some of these poems first appeared: *Arc Poetry Magazine, The Canadian Forum, Prism international, Germination, Gaspereau Review, Pottersfield Portfolio, 1979-80,* and *The Literary Review of Canada. Yet at a Distance: Father Poems from the Maritimes.* Gary Burrill, editor. 2008. Ottawa: Borealis Press. *Coastlines, The Poetry of Atlantic Canada.* Anne Compton et al., editors. 2002. Fredericton: Goose Lane Editions; *Landmarks, An Anthology of New Atlantic Canadian Poetry of the Land.* Hugh MacDonald and Brent MacLaine, editors. 2001. Charlottetown: The Acorn Press; *Poetic Voices of the Maritimes, A Selection of Contemporary Poetry.* Allison Mitcham and Theresia Quigley, editors. 1996. Hantsport, Nova Scotia: Lancelot Press; *Reconcilable Differences, The Changing Face of Poetry by Canadian Men since 1970.* Christopher Levenson, editor. 1994. Calgary: Bayeux; *The Atlantic Anthology, Volume 2/Poetry.* Fred Cogswell, editor. 1985. Charlottetown: Ragweed Press; *Prism international, 25 Years in Retrospect.* John Shoutsen and St. John Simmons, editors. 1984. Vancouver: Department of Creative Writing, University of British Columbia; and *Chezzetcook, An Anthology of Contemporary Poetry and Fiction from Atlantic Canada.* Lesley Choyce, editor. 1978. Halifax: Wooden Anchor Press.

"Revelations" was performed in February, 1984, by Nightwood Theatre in Toronto under the direction of Michael Fuller. "Poet's Fields" was broadcast on CBC Radio. "Atlantic Elegy" was commissioned by *Canadian Geographic* for *Through The Lens, 1998 Annual*.

The epigraph for "Grist" in "Greenfields & Grist" is taken from "Winter in Durnover Field" by Thomas Hardy.

The epigraph for "Of Elms and Men" is taken from Robert Francis' poem, "The Fate of Elms."

Epigraph for "Record of a Weather-Exposed Skeleton" is taken from Matsuo Basho's "The Records of A Weather-Exposed Skeleton" in *The Narrow Road To The Deep North and Other Travel Sketches*. 1987. trans. Nobuyuki Yuasa. Penguin Books Ltd., England.

Epigraph for "The Owl and The Fox" is taken from Tomas Tranströmer in *The Spell of the Sensuous, Perception and Language in a More-Than-Human World*. 1996. Abram, David. Pantheon Books, New York.

Epigraph for "Pacific Odes, 3. Ode To The Marine Iguana" is taken from Herman Melville's short story, "The Encantadas."

In "Iris: Epithalamium," the line *"darkness starting up where she stood, the night coming through her eyes"* is taken from D.H. Lawrence's poem, "A Young Wife."

Quotes by John Ruskin in *A Ship Portrait* are taken from Ruskin's *Modern Painters*.

Quotes by Elizabeth Bishop in "Geography: On First Discovering Elizabeth Bishop In A Used Bookstore in Manhattan" are taken from her poem "The Moose" and her stories "Primer Class," "The Country Mouse," and "In The Village."

The author owes a debt to Derek Walcott's poem, "The Sea Is History," for the first line of "Atlantic Elegy, 3. Black Hull."

Barefaced Stone

[1980]

The Old Order

for M. & K.

No longer exists,
must be unearthed,

cleaved free, as amethyst
from dull stone, crystalline

at the sea's edge:

then the contemporaneous
recedes, becomes vestigial

like the leathery wort
once the equine fifth toe.

Anvil, axe and rein
join voice with heron and raven,

lit by coronas
of old stars and coal oil.

Pasture Rock Prodigy

I tell you, before coming to this country,
I would not have believed it myself,
that rocks copulate, bear children—
no matter how many you roll away,
there will be twice that again,
come spring. What else
are you to believe!

In November: the sky still stagnant pond,
clouds strung like frogs' eggs,
inchoate black life wriggling at the centre,
stones swell as if gestating.

Ask the old people, they will tell you
of the shamelessness of stones.
But if you should show telltale sign
of disbelief or disgust,
they will pretend not to have meant it.
Like their grandfathers who told them,
when they were but children,
they will laugh, take pity,
try to pass it off as a joke.

Greenfields & Grist

for John Mildon

I. Greenfields

> Greenfield: The name is descriptive...
> —*Place Names and Places of Nova Scotia*

Greenfield: not as prosaic
as it may sound, for where
was one to be found that first year
in this place of mast trees?
It was for them (as it is for me now)
a declaration of faith,
and through the first winter,
of doubt. The bulb
burning above my desk,
no brighter than the sun
in February, fine vapours
of light filtering in my window,
mingling with my smoke,
my heat. Where is one
to be found? The view
short-circuited by a barbed wire fence,
the bottleneck of a grizzled apple tree:
amnesia sets in. Try to picture
the field as green, a bright festive
green, not the never-quite-green
of the softwoods: the eye disparages.
This name agrees with the senses
one quarter of the year—
in summer, the prosaic season.

ii. Grist

Rook. —Throughout the field I find no grain;
The cruel frost encrusts the cornland!
—Thomas Hardy

Scratch the cross-hatched pane,
face February,
bear the weight
of this month's millstone.

In this country's cycle
one returns within himself,
winter to winter.
Stone against bone we are reduced,
the meal of our fortune is scattered
treeline to fencepost.

Men are the harvest here:
scapula, ulna, femur and skull,
their husk cracked,
kernel of marrow ground
to one consistency.

Crows (snow devils'
black loci)
cavil over the spoils.

Straw Men

Their season is over:
in the stubble
the bone-amber stooks
lie among the ribcages
of archaic rakes,
phalanges of forks
that have hefted
their last load.
I pity them a little:
today begins a month of Sundays,
the smell of wood
takes them by the throat,
the sky shivers so
its gleaming teeth
fall from its head.
I pity them a little:
their strange harvest.

Sanctuary

for Joseph Basaraba

He bent solitary to subtle tasks in still nights
—*The Microbe Hunters*

Under the professor's clinical cloak,
you retain the habit and heart
of your father's peasant stock.
When not fastened over a microscope lens,
sizing up a virulent world in miniature,
you culture benign missiles: zucchini,
cucumber and squash. Substitute manure
for the agar of horse's marrow,
the scent of blossoms for the bacilli's effluvium.

Overhead, the politicians of pollen buzz
flower to flower—a gentle anarchy.
Underfoot the long night of the worm
works its miracle of loam.
The acidic earth eats to the heart of a man,
the spade overturns civilizations.

Knowing this, we seek sanctuary,
a place where 'a man can keep his head
while others around him are losing their's'.
Kipling's commandments, resurrected
from your undergraduate files
for a bearded student you called Moses.

Joseph, I remember your lectures,
limned with Polish proverbs:
*When a stranger walks through town
the dogs bark.*
History's footnotes:
Nazis goosestepped over your villages.
Soviet tanks left their reptilian track.

On the new continent, you laugh blackly
as Conrad, spin your tale leisurely
as Marlowe. Yet the students yelp
for a whelp of facts, are eager
to take inventory of the material world.

Man is a strange *animacule.* Leeuwenhoek,
fussily polishing his monocle,
logging the antics in a droplet's pond,
the beasties resident in his tooth scum,
discovering, in fact: we are never alone.

Clouds Flying Before the Eye

(1985)

Stoney Island

for Ron Smith

Between scrub and bedrock
no place for the plough,
a constant curling of water,
men depart by boat or causeway
to return at nightfall if at all.

To think: this could have been ours,
granite in the green Atlantic,
but for a drowning and tuberculosis.
Only disaster wrenches men away
from such destiny.

It is as if our fathers,
our grandfathers had never left.
Its barrenness inhabits us still.
Can you see a Cape Island boat
without wanting to steer it to her source?
This urge so strong, we wish to reclaim
what we have never possessed,
what other men believe is not worth having.

Poet's Fields

It has been a good year
for old fruit. Strawberries
wakened in the hay field
among clover and timothy,
full, sweet as when
they were planted.
It is the same
with these raspberries
—old canes cut down
and forgotten, this summer
have risen up
and borne big fruit.
It is a small miracle.
I celebrate it
even though the fields
are a riot of purple vetch,
daisies and goldenrod
—a poet's fields,
not those of a good farmer
with stock to feed.
I am glad to glean.
I do not give back much
—these few words.
Still no practical man
wants this hill to call
his own any longer.
I might as well be here
to remember what men
have done, their old labours.
Seeing me through summer's heat,
green canes to my shoulders,
straw hat on my head,
intent on my Sunday pleasure,
who can tell I am not one of them
come up from the earth
to renew it?

June Bugs

What do they want anyway—
battering against the clapboard
like kamakazes?
Burdened with armour
their flight is erratic.
Spluttering our of dew-laden grass
they manage a brief
excursion into night,
then crash noisily.
In the morning
their wrecked fuselages
litter the verandah
like unpleasant lozenges
that had been spit out.

But let's be honest.
It is not their manner
that bothers us most.
It is the message they bear
as they burst from their earth crypts
into summer air:
This is June
long awaited
short lived.

Surfaces

I.

Fish head
hen fish
metallic blue
bright, bloody
spectacle
in the stainless
steel sink.

You look down into the deep pool
of your domestic world,
images rise up,
            muscular,
breaking the surface tension
        of the everyday,
                    arcing into spectra.

This was your youngest son's first salmon.
You looked down (a knife in your hands)
there it was—

a gut thing for the eye, art,

disembodied,
stripped of its family of meaning.

II.

Salmon draw me to riverbanks.
I stand for days working a line.
In the end the hooked fish
brings me to my knees.

There is no more pleasure
in tethering beauty
than in glimpsing it.

Finally I expect
it is only important
to know where beauty

lies: tensed silver
below the blinding surface.

Revelations

For God's sake
come up out of the cellar—
the world I tell you
is not going to end in the morning.

Neither with thunder nor fire—
that's the vision of boy children
their pale necks chafed red
by their starched collars.

This is how the world ends
if you want to know:
I go out one morning
to feed my bullcalf.

And as I always do
I get down on my hunkers
to watch and listen
to him feed awhile.

His snout flecked
with the grain
he looks up, sees me
slumped down—asleep.

And in the whole great sounding box
of the barn, there is only
the music of his soft face
in the trough.

The Stammerer's Soliloquy

There are times I can't even understand
myself for this damn stammering.
It is only here in this tarred shack
I can say something straight out
like I hear in my head.
This dog listens—right, boy—after all
we gnaw on the same fucking bone.
My neighbour, what does he know
for all his learning?
I'll not stutter my courtesy,
blurt it out for his sake today.
I'll step where I please.

Damn that bitch of his,
always at my heels,
why can't he keep it tied?
Can't I walk the ground without that?
I'll keep my complaint to myself,
silence serves me best, as they say.
Then, God, I'll have enough of it—
it can't come too soon.

If Men Lived on Earth

[2000]

Northing

for J. H., 1888-1991

North, tending like a compass needle,
now that it is summer, field season.
Labrador, James or Hudson Bay, New Found Land,
places where the sagas were played out, or here,
Cape Breton Island, where the north woods begin.
Rock poking through, a lake looking up, and trees,
darker, thinner the farther north one wanders.
Look down, it's hard to know what land this is,
whose name it has taken, who in a fit of hubris,
of exhilaration at making it this far,
over mountains and plains of the sea,
claimed it for some unclean, parochial sovereign.

Most roads have no hardtop—black tar
our Nazca lines from which the future will reinvent us,
our obsession with mere movement—
most are woods' roads ending in desolation.
For absentee landlords we are still hacking the woods back,
clearcuts our 20th-century Clearances.
Then one morning capital flees to slash and burn
        somebody else's country,
leaving us to start over again.

How many times have we begun? Below, a road
the woods nearly have healed over, a single cellar
in a clearing—another story without an ending.
Look down and remember: one hundred and four years ago,
a daughter was born to a shipping broker on this island.
A woman of fierce, closed pride, a memory keeper,
a spinster we admired but could not mellow.
Even death found her difficult: her stubbornness
kept him waiting, *too long,* we, the living, glibly said.

Near the end, she was bearded, her skin
a palimpsest scripted with blue veins,
the skeleton pressing out
like the tea-stained bones of Basque whalers at Red Bay,
the pitiful remains of arctic exploits preserved in peat.
Look down: a road in the forest, a cellar,
the remembrance of an old woman,
some bones in a northern land I keep re-discovering
as I follow the curve of the earth in season—northing.

Terrarium

Passed over the table like a fruit bowl,
a cranium smooth as beach stone. Palming it,
despite myself, I think of my wife,
how she likes to have her head caressed.

I think of her, too, because you say
the skull was found in the barren ground—
and she shares the broad, high cheekbones
with this people who crossed over the world's roof.

The skull's sutures knit hemispheres,
as does old Mother Earth,
her lands one island before the slow drift
marooned us on continents.

We travel to become whole again. I drift
from New World Islands down on the Labrador
where her people and those of this hollow soul
met and mixed, if only in my imagination.

The spirit of this skull was nomadic once,
pivoted, surveyed the earth's circumference.
Now it is helpless, passed between hands
as lovingly as a newborn. But look—

Orange lichen grows inside the skull's bowl.
Even in death, the earth lives on within us.

Of Elms and Men

Though elms must die, not everything must die
        −Robert Francis

Our fate is not theirs, so you say,
or is it? Like men, elms die from the top down,
undone by some lowly contagion
under their skin. Greed, hubris, naïveté.

Once lordly, leafing over waters and pastures,
they anchored the landscape. Now skeletal,
they remind us of time's flow, the unstoppable
disappearance of things, one by one, year by year,

a measure of our own shallow hold on the earth.
Some day, lodged in the mud where a river once swelled
will be minerals, stone where once there were cells.
All that will remain to say there was something of worth.

Our fate is not theirs, so you say−
Or is it? Like elms, men die from the top down.

Record Of A Weather-Exposed Skeleton

for Geoffrey Cook

Determined to fall
A weather-exposed skeleton
I cannot help the sore wind
Blowing through my heart.
    —Basho

Already the hay is tinged red, the flowers
my daughter picked last week are dry
in the vase. In the afternoon, the blinds
remain three-quarters drawn. Yesterday
I waded the river, letting the dark water
carry away my weariness. On the bank
what did I find but vertebrae
shaped like soaring birds—
if held to the lips they might make
hollow flute sounds—
a skull, long and equine, the knowing mask
of some Greek tragedy. A moose skeleton, whole,
articulated, as if the old animal had come to drink
and simply laid down and died
to a single, mournful note.
Or, to symphonic music,
had been run down to the water's edge,
its great rack swinging wildly in the charged air.
At dusk an owl glided through the tree tops,
a pack of wild dogs yipped in the shadows
as if they smelled blood.
I walked out of the woods at dark. Exhausted,
I sleep past noon. Now, the images of the day before
return, hard and clean as bone.
I listen to the brittle stirrings of the grasses
outside the bedroom window. Down the hall,
the little song of my daughter's voice in the playroom.

Just now, she has picked up a plastic harmonica
and begun to play a tune
the world has never heard before.

Chimney Swifts

for Catherine

Fly ash, swifts swirl counter-
clockwise around the chimney

*like smoke returning
to the fire.* Time's arrow

is reversed. As we watch their flight
spiral into darkness,

we are growing younger,
back toward our births,

borne to our mother's womb
on charcoal wings.

First one bravely dips
into the inky stack,

then the others
obediently funnel down

to the mystery of our origins.
A place still, dark, expectant.

Dusk, the show is over,
we file obediently toward our appointment

with sleep, resume our steady movement
no longer suspended by waking wonder.

In the morning, the flock
unwinds like clock springs,

flies up as if the night foreman
had returned, kindled old fires.

The swifts, winged carbon, spiral up,
clockwise at the dawn light,

setting the day in motion,
unfurling the future.

Flowers Of Love: Three Prose Poems

i. Lupine

That such an exotic thing should run riot on the roadsides is unnorthern. Its spires of purple, pink and blue are a mixture of all colours of passion, gathered into an upthrusting of energy from earth to air, an energy at once carnal and spiritual. Individual blossoms each pushed out on their own handles look like baby prams. Then, too, each is as delicately veined, as transparent, as an old woman's skin. Blooms spiral around the stem which is curved tautly with purpose, like the penis bones of sea mammals, the laboured pleasure of their breeding muffled by the sound of surf. The leaves bristling with a hairy down, like a young woman's forearm, seem almost tropical in their fierce perfection. Rousseau, walrus-mustachioed custom's clerk, might have imagined lupine in his innocent world of jungle and noble humans uninspired by an urge to civilization. Lupine line our roadsides like the phosphorescence of the sea pushed aside by a prow seeking someplace not yet a colony.

ii. Violets

They grow in damp places where waters have risen dropwise to overflowing as if a faucet had been left on all night. The blossom is blue or purple or violet, no one seems to be able to say for sure—perhaps because the colour is so unexpected and hypnotically dark like a storm cloud interjecting itself suddenly upon a cloudless sky. The blossom hangs from a green shepherd's crook planted into the swampy earth with authority. It has five petals. Two perk up like a mongrel's ears. Three hang down, and the central one might be a spout, the tongue of a gargoyle spilling rainwater from the eaves of a gothic cathedral. The dignity of this little flower is heraldic, demands to be restated. In watercolour would be best, for it springs from water as do all things: waters of the earth, waters of mothers,

Christ in the form of a fish. As a child I knew damp places to kneel and pick a fistful of violets for my mother. No other flower so perfectly made the innocent correspondence between the things of life I most loved.

III. Iris: Epithalamium

Snake flowers I called them as a five-year-old, fearing biblical serpents, thunder-headed, coiled in the damp pools where the irises grew. Blue flags they are called, signifying the country of backwaters, of idleness where rainbows of oil collect. Formally, iris, of the eye, the prism of colour sun-bursting there at the entrance to the mind. Your eyes: 'Nothing grows without looking into them,' I wrote, your young lover afraid as Lawrence of his young wife when he wrote of the *darkness starting up where she stood, the night coming through her eyes.* A year later we stood among the iris to marry, blue-eyed witnesses at our feet. Me in my purple tweed suit, you with purple art nouveau flowers twining around your thighs. At land's end, the place where Africa drifted away, we vowed our love under the eye of the lighthouse, fog swirling around us in ecstatic atomic dervishes.

Three sets of three petals gather inward, toward the dark centre. The stamen is cleverly concealed to unleash its seed. The sulphurous throat of the petals like the incandescence under a thunderhead makes the heart jump. I never see these flowers without repeating our love. Looking into the iris's eye, holding its fibrous taut stem, I think of entrances, the continents sliding away and bumping together again— for all time.

The Owl And The Mouse

The wild does not have words...
Language, but no words.
        —Tomas Tranströmer

In February, a feral alphabet: a thin line
of mouse tracks scribbled across the flawless powder,
intersecting it, the signature of attack // caesura.
Two lives met here, one, light-footed, earthbound,
the other, aerial, heavy-winged. Two lines
drawn together by hunger. On impact, the owl made
angel wings, white and perfect as the living body,
every feather, every barbule, printed in the new snow.
Two lines on the page of winter
tell a simple story, in simple language, not words:
Two lives met here, became one.

River Otters At Play

Love
as it ought to be made:
leisurely, buoyant, liquid.
The river otters roll
over, the male a hapless sailor
holding hard to the capsizing
keel of the female.
Over
       and under
they sink,
bubbling desire, emerge
       au pair
sucking night air,
circling together,
       clasped
one to the other—
otter to otter.

Love as play,
in this they are always
faithful and true.
Love made as such things
ought to be done, with grace,
       for fun.
I have seen them before,
not locked like this,
but moving free,
       in synchrony
dive and surface together,
anxious to spy the other's face—
okay, they say, and dive again,
weaving their submarine passions.
Or on the slippery bank,
       slide

over the other's oily back,
musking each other
as they enter water,
each quick, sleek movement
a kind of foreplay,
sensing the other's wet wishes.
Now they are in no hurry;
as the light fails
they court the dark waters,
stirring them,
and, deep down,
limbic me.

Arcadia: The Marsh Suite

1. Tidal River

I have returned—
to *Great-still-water,*

Che-bo-gue, calm as a clock
at the turning of the tide,

black spruce, crow-crowned
totems mirrored in its face.

This is the view through a camera:
image turned on its head—

time, too. This is the place
of childhood transposed.

Here I am again,
an eye still rejoicing

at the flat, green world
leavened with salt.

2. Marsh

Unkempt fertility: greenness, wetness,
sudden depths—sink holes to swallow
the body of a five-year-old—
darkness from which there was no exit.

Unmanned acres: a collection place for salt,
driftwood, jetsam, dead cats and living birds;
patens, mattress grass soft underfoot,
a carpet of summer dreams without foreboding.

On the marsh, there was only the willet
to scold me: "*Kip, kip, kip,*" each note
more strident, as if I were a fox kit
too playfully close to its saltwater nest.

Pit-a-wee, we called this boundary drawer,
inscribing circles of sound around our world.
The red heart of the creek at its centre
pumped moon-drawn wonder—systole, diastole.

Heron was the timekeeper, the "S" of the neck
funnelled darkness into its grey weight.
Shitepoke, its poker legs rammed in at the back,
flew low over the marsh, nighttime its freight.

3. Staddles

Strings of an aeolian harp,
all that remained to tell us
we were not the first
to people these green pastures of the sea.
In my matinee version of history,
they were scaffolds for the Indian dead,
crows had carried off their bones long ago,
leaving only the wind to speak of absence.
Invisible as the wind, those others before us:
their whetted scythes whispering through *spartina,*
they mounded the horse hay on the staddle,
fingers of a great hand
reaching up to a New World god.
But I could not hear the old man's oxcart,
hobbling, heavy-wheeled, across the frozen dykeland,
could not see him fork winter fodder
tinged with salt and iodine—
like the syllables spilling from his tongue,
a rich mingling of elements
the sea had washed ashore.
I could not see the civilizations
stacked one on top of the other,
bound together by the lattice of clay
the tide let down daily.
There was only the wind,
speaking its ever-living language,
corrugations of green light
passing through my skinny ribs
            without a sound.

4. Tide Pool

Pond scum, like a cow's hide,
hollow without its animal inside;
limp with no cage of bone
      to hang upon.

Pulp of marsh grass,
fabric of cells,
a sacred archives
waits for meaning–

flourish of bullrush:
Ideogram.

4. Wood Duck

At the pond muddling for minnows
I looked behind, suddenly aware
of the watcher— there, perched in alder,
was the wood duck. A Noh play actor
with its green warrior's helmet,
white facial lines pencilled on
like those of an ancient mandarin.
Back and breast anointed in irreverent purples,
visceral maroons, metallic flashes of iridescence
like dragon flies embroidered in silk lamé—
such an oriental extravagance in the grey world
       of drab April!

I did not quite believe it to be a bird,
but an altered reality winged as angels.
Reverence hushed my breathing, stillness
strained to hold its beauty;
then I moved and the bird vanished,
as if a tree hole were the portal
to another world,
some brightness beyond nature.

5. Mummichog

With heron-stealth, I tiptoe, slink
to the tide pool's edge, taking care
not to throw shadow, telegraph sound.
There, darting under the colloidal cloud
of pond scum, hides the mummichog,
fat minnow, rough-skinned as carp.
(I want it for the clear water
of my mayonnaise jar.) It dives out of reach
of my unheron-like strike,
stirring a puff of sediment
as it buries its rotundness in mud—
a mistake. I plunge to my armpit,
clutching bottom, feel the beating mummichog,
cold heart in my hand, deposit dirt and all
            into my vessel.
A small life swims round and round,
its world shrunk, fatally simplified.
This thumb-sized roughneck,
yogi of the pond, can survive
the storm's dilution, the sun's merciless drying
at the neaps, even winter's ice,
but not a boy's naive wonder,
his need to possess.

6. Elver

I lift each streambed rock with care,
grab sand, a grit of mineral
flashing in the sun. Something leaps
alive in my hand, like a sperm tail
beating at the womb's door.
Eel, trying to slither free,
find egress through the portcullis
          of fingers.
I nab the translucent hybrid
of fish and snake, half at home on land
where it may migrate in season.
Its visible backbone runs
its little length, like lead
in a yellow pencil, a line
alternately wavy and straight,
as it writes its panic on my palm.
I snap off its head between thumbnail
and index fat— the long sea road
to the Sargasso is severed.
Lay out the day's catch
on a flat stone, like a Basque
preserving his winter's store
on a spruce-bough flake, four-hundred years before.
Seeing the eel dry in the sun, the boy
feels the thin pale line—electric!
arcing through his own supple spine.

7. Smelts

Nocturnal predators, we slipped
dark as mink toward saltwater,
flicking on the flashlight only long enough
to spot the moving mass of fins and fish eyes.

Plenty, in spring, to kneel in the cold earth,
plunge bare hands into the numbing dark,
feel the hairy scales of distant seas brush by.

We snatched them, alive, over our shoulder
until the hands, arthritic with cold,
seined nothing but water.
Or we scooped them in a net jury-rigged
from an onion bag, hoop and alder.

Happy, we toted home sagging burlap.
Mother scissored open bellies,
spilling the milt and spawn into a basin.

The stove, stoked too high for April nights,
made the kitchen delirious with heat.
The room filled with onomatopoeia.

Their white flesh was sacrament,
the pale body of spring
unburdened of ice.
We ate with the abandon of nomads, free
to walk the earth, foraging in season.

Weeks later, I overturned rocks—
the delicate corpses of spent lovers
floated up, frayed where the gut
had released its seed. Twisting
            in the current,
the dead slid downstream

in a slow, dreadful ballet,
while in the gravel, dark eyes blinked,
illuminated by the yellow sun of a yolk sac
hanging from the fingerling's spine
like a storm lantern from a lightkeeper's hand.

8. Heron

Still here, watching
the watcher.

Lift your wings, nimbus
rising over the Atlantic—

and the heart lifts too.

You are the overseer of tall grasses,
spartina and sedges,

a tangle of driftwood,
up and walking.

Out for a stroll, you turn
the marsh into murderer's row

as you pluck one, then another,
with appalling aplomb.

To be that still,
inert as mineral,

to wait, stalwart,
without weariness,

staring down the barrel
of your beak, eyes

balanced like pince-nez
reading depth.

Drawing back the serpentine neck,
hunched between clavicles,

you uncoil, scissor
the silver stickleback.

Thoth of the marsh, pained writer
picking his way, knees bent,

syllable by syllable,
through the shallows

of silence. Working
a single pool

for every silvery
twitching prize—

the fuel of grey flight.
Lift your nimbus wings—

and the heart lifts too.

Apocrypha

1. Any writings, anecdotes, etc. of doubtful authenticity
or authorship... 3. various writings falsely attributed
to Biblical characters or kept out of the New Testament
as not genuine.

1. Genesis

The Bluebird Motel,
rented happiness above the tide,
its name a pun on my maker.
How did I begin?
Fathered of dancing,
drunkenly forgetting the War,
each man with his own reason,
one who had gone, one who stayed home.
Survivors, arms around each other,
staggering among the gravestones,
propped next to one, bootleg rum.
Voices rose above the tide
as best friends danced
with each others's wives.
But when it was time for bed
my mother hooked my father's arm.
They rocked like a moored boat
as I swam through their salt waters
          toward time.

2. Family Tree

My father, it's said,
could not bear to look at my nakedness—
too much colour, features forceps flattened—

so when my mother bathed me,
he escaped to the woods.
Family apocrypha, I say.

Looking, what would he have seen?
Not the disappointment of late sown seed,
            simply more necessity.

He packed double-bitted axe and crosscut
            for the woodlot,
for a man in March, the only place of labour.
            Even there
my voice rose like sap into hungry branches.

3. Christian Name

Harry, a poet's name? "No!" I hear
my grandfather raise his objection
from the grave, "A horse's name!"
Sound echoed along Pleasant Street,
a straight line struck on a flat iron.
Truck drivers unloaded balsa boxes,
the smell of fruit drifting overripe
into the nostril of memory.
The ice cart left its cool stain
in the dust; I crammed my mouth
full of cold crystal (even then
having begun the poet's small job
of remembering how it feels.)

Way back before I can remember,
a milkman, kisses of glass
in his wire basket, walks ahead
of wagon and horse, "Get up, Harry!"
His voice passed like stinging gossip
along the street, making granddad redden,
years later deny my brother his Christian name.
But when it came to me,
his last chance for a namesake,
his pride weakened in the face of oblivion—
obediently, I pull the name of a horse
        into the future.

4. Adam

Pain stabbed under my ribs
as I conformed to the palette
of my first school desk.
I communed with fear
in the curtained room,
shouting my parent's names
into the echoic halls
until sleep silenced me.
The next morning, I entered ether—
a sweet place of distant voices—
counting my new learned numbers backward.
The masked man reached into my side,
plucked out a worm,
an unfinished bit of creation,
an idea pinched off.

(Perhaps this vermiform organ
is not what it appears
to be, an appendix,
but a source that long ago elongated,
looped upon itself,
eventually sprouting soft tissues,
bone, blood, brain— words.
It inflames to remind us
of our beginnings.)

Like Adam I now had a scar,
first visible memory
that shone on my abdomen
like a petroglyph on a cave wall.

5. Little Jesus

Barely five feet tall,
the old man, his white Afro
spiraling in the sun like a halo,
opened the doors of the box
built onto the back of his pick-up
and out rolled the sea,
"Any flesh fish, today, lady?"
his tongue clinging to the back
of his rotten teeth, rum upon his breath.

Haddock and hake, the silvered skin
clinging to the white flesh,
amber of finnan haddie,
whiskered cod or dried cod
hanging up, an old sea incarnate.
Or my favourite fish, mackerel,
chevrons of blue and magenta
from the sharp-forked tail
to the dead but still-looking pupil.

"Are they fresh?" mother asks
suspiciously.

"Flesh today, lady. A few hours ago
they was swimming in the sea."

Mother brings a porcelain basin,
places the mackerel, sacrificially,
in a shallow pool of their own blood.

Then Little Jesus— so-called
for his wild prophet's look—
battens the doors
and takes the sea with him
down our lane.

There was no man I wished to be like
more than him, his hooks in the sea,
his eyes always on horizons.
If I could I would have followed.

6. Old Testament

The family stood in solemn circle
as he raised the rope hand over hand,
with dry glance measured our ration,
tied a new knot closer to the rock plumb.

July, August, brothers took bars of soap
with their swimming trunks to bathe in the creek.
As days peeled off the calendar parched
as onion skins, we waited his conversion.

My brother and I watched as his figure
became smaller, then paler, finally
disappeared below the muddy creek bank
as below the gunwales of a baptistry.

We laughed stitches, knowing his hatred
of unheated water. But when his body
appeared again, a white birthmark
on the russet land, we put away our glee,

fearing our father would come rolling
across the marsh, dark and dangerous,
like a god clothed in a thunder cloud
                to avenge our blasphemy.

7. Our Fathers In Heaven

"Lay a hand on me and I'll kill you," I said,
stopping father in his tracks. He didn't laugh,
though I don't doubt he wanted to, seeing my defiant
five-year-old frame blocking his way.
For a moment he must have wished
I was a grown man,
he could strike me
with all his strength. Instead
he walked away, leaving me alone
with the wretchedness of words.

In the Bible
fathers sacrificed sons.
Abraham took his only son
to the mountain, tied him like a goat
to the altar. God himself gave
his only son to mankind.
Men nailed him to a tree.

I feared my father, though
he had never struck me
nor would he ever. I feared
his able carpenter's hands
with their deltas of dirt,
orange thumbnails,
an eighth-inch thick,
the reek of tobacco rising from our pew
like incense in a more catholic church.

In the end, we learn, it is not presence
but absence we must fear most.
I held his soft hands,
as day after day he grew lighter,
until they became wings
for his hollowed body.

Pacific Odes

1. Ode To A Pacific Fishing Boat

for Kelly Kellogg

This boat is like the Pacific,
its yellow gunwales are the rim
of the sailor's world,
a mauve monotony
of rising and setting
suns. Its blue hull
bobbing above an abyss of words,
the hue of India ink,
records the ceaseless swells,
a line scrawled over and over
across the *mare incognita*
of maps.

See how happily the Rapa Nui apply
the paint, imagining
a harvest of octopuses,
puffer fish, the horse-red
meat of bonito,
its heart skewered
by a spear gun's lance
as if by a jealous
lover.

Neruda would have loved this pacific boat,
its happy unamerican family, its succulent
enterprise of sea creatures;
the green breakers, brown boys holding
their manes, riding ashore;
the shrouded benevolence of the women's hips,
a keel and water
in commotion.

Neruda would have praised such a scene,
his heart gaping wide as the ocean
he faced daily. Proud figurehead
of a worm-eaten ship,
salvaging beauty,
oddity—perhaps the same thing—
in the binnacle
of his eye.

2. Ode To The Marine Iguana

> Little but reptile life is found here...
> No voice, no low, no howl is heard; the
> chief sound of life here is a hiss.
> —Herman Melville,

Out of the mouth of the Andes
issued the lisping waters
flushing flotsam into the endless Pacific.
Rafts of deadwood eddied westward
and on the poop deck, riding high,
the admiral of the castaways,
your reptilian crest
peaked as Horatio's cock-eyed hat.
It was perhaps then
you first learned to eat
the sea's salad,
blow salt from your nose,
tearful geysers bleaching
your head like snow
atop an extinct volcano.
Was it then, on your maiden voyage,
you first had an inkling to crawl
back into the womb
of Mother Sea
while all else was crawling out?

Perhaps you tired of life on land
and headed out one day
thinking never to return.
But you could not forsake
the sun, the earth, so came ashore
to bask and converse
in that dry dead language
known only to your kind.

Each morning I find you
sprawled on my patio,
black as lava
except for your halo
of halide.
Stupid and hideous,
the young Darwin declared,
and catching you by the tail
hurled you like a ball
and chain
                       into a tidepool
where you sulked,
then shuffled away
at the indignity
of it all.

Over breakfast
I watch you jousting
for position,
head to head,
like the chivalrous
knights of old.
Or a pair of Sumo wrestlers
observing ritual,
you bow three times
before butting heads,
each trying to drive
the other back
into the sea.

Why do you cling so
desperately to the rocks
if the sea is your second home?
Perhaps like all sailors,
casting off, you long
for the mountains
of land,

and shorebound,
look longingly
to the mountains
of the sea?
Then, grizzled one,
you have more answers than me.
Magellan
of the reptiles,
you have mastered
the trick of turning
time itself on its
hoary head.

3. Ode To the Giant Tortoises

Original clay
petrified,
your pace is geological,
patient.
Once the world balanced
on your backs,
now you teeter
on your black islands
of oblivion.

Melville and his mates
made soup tureens
of your carapaces,
having first sucked out
your sweet flesh,
giving thanks
for the respite from salt meat.

You there, four-hundred-pounder,
might have stretched your leathery
    .   neck
like a puppeteer's sock
to inquire after Darwin
in his youth—
and not despised him,
then or now.

You, of all beings,
shared his genius:
change comes slowly,
tortoise-wise;
knowing this, you transformed
your domed house
into a saddle.

Homesick sailors boarded you,
a terrestrial barquentine,
rolled and pitched
to an ancient rhythm.
Decades later, dying
within the roar
of glacial seas,
remembered that one tropical
miracle,
riding atop your humped self,
mounded earth,
as if touched
by the cuticle
of God.

And now you too
are comic old men
without heirs.
Grunt, belch and wheeze;
jungle juices
foam about your beaks,
dribble down
your chins.

Men, boiling under the rusted roofs
of the Equator,
stomp ashore on the islands
named for you,
the original Galapagueño.
You have witnessed this pageant before:
madmen, starving or glutted
with ambition,
become prisoners here.

In hunger and in spite
they have overturned your world,
torn out its soft underbelly,

hacked off its head.
You forgive them,
fixing them with the rime
of your time-weary eyes.
You pity them
their short lives,
their short sight.

4. Ode To A Red-billed Tropic Bird

Half-way, neither here nor there.
Heavy seas, the keel cutting the slopes
of moving mountains—over, over!
Flying fish buzz from the wave crests
like a child's wind-up toys; then,
this bosun's whistle startles us awake,
the sibilance of seabird talk
like air expressed through tooth-gaps.
Chanteclers of the sea
circle the crosstrees, trail
the cock-like pride of their forked tails
that, backlit, look more like bridal veils.

This is the pale shape of our loneliness,
thin as wisps of breath fluttering in our wake.
Absences. Another living thing, warm-blooded
anything out here is sacred, kin, even this ghostly bird.
Inside us is this like spark, crimsoned by the trades.

Out here, all birds are Coleridge's albatross.
Rejoice in their presence, or hang sorrow,
rotting, around your neck the live-long day.
Hold wonder in your eye, they sing,
or sail alone, always.

Atlantic Elegy

1. The Salt

I admit it, perhaps only a poet
could love the Atlantic's sombre palette:
shale grey, bilge green, milt blue; the blood-red
of sky in the sailor's rhyme, memorizing
the horizon's warning or delight.
The constant companionship of fog,
a sibling presence, a kind of tide clock,
mantra of sea breath always billowing
from the harbour's mouth; the diaphone,
mythic, half-human, half-animal,
a Minotaur tethered at land's end,
bellowing day and night. The gull's
perfect flight, precise as origami,
floating up from the fish-mongering docks.
The thrum of marine diesel, tap of slant-six
salvaged from some rust-eaten wreck. The salt.
The smell of the sea floor—Georges
or Grand Banks, Banquereau, even Sable's sands
shuffling beneath our feet on Water Street.

11. Blue Geography

Passages, islands, coves, tickles and guts—
the jigsaw of our blue geography:

Earth womb, heaviness at the warm centre
pushed out, lifted up for all to see.
Heat of the living planet, since cooled
and time worn. The thin cloak of coastal green
a living lesson of the miracle
come out of the sea, the deep vents
        of the living Earth.

Even the whale-back rocks appear alive,
breaching the waves, advancing ashore
following some ancient map, some compass
        needle at their warm core.

Old mountains tumble into the sea,
the flare of fall maples a mere spark
of Appalachia, the ring of fire arching
        over the old Atlantic.

The long ride of waves from the Outer Islands—
Templars, priests and paupers, so much flotsam
on their backs—breaks against the mantle
        of the New World.

New and old locked in a slow quadrille,
quick jig or reel, joined on a shingle beach,
the long sigh, soughing withdrawal, shore
        to long shore.

Abegweit, cradled by the waves, the Island
ochre-red, a living colour. Middens
of oyster shells, a calendar of calcium,
piled up in seasons of plenty. Sea cows

stirred the cove bottoms with their gleaming tusks
planted into the shallows like two-tyned forks.

Walrus and people shared the harvest
until sails and guns appeared in the Gulf,
eyeglass and sextant imposed an Old World
vision. The garden on land and sea
was cross-hatched by harrow and bottom trawl.

Now the old desert sandstone, graveyard
of mountains, is lapped with salt, rasped
smooth by the sea's tongue, the idle footfalls
of come-from-aways, urban refugees
seeking a place rendered simple by water
                    and wind.

Mussel-blue islands, one for each day
of the year, now harbour freestone cellars,
eyeless lighthouses, the guttural of gulls.
Islands like the capsized hulls of ships,
cat spruce scuttling on their barnacled bellies
like the survivors of some nameless wreck.

iii. Black Hull

The sea is memory. Forests of masts
growing in the harbours, white pine with sails
for leaves, reefed, expectant as held breath.
Every mud creek bed cradled a keel,
every ocean hailed a bluenose captain,
every parlour blossomed with the exotic,
every roof top sprouted a widow's walk;
sail lofts, foundries, insurance houses
stitched, hammered and brokered maritime dreams.
Then, black clouds smudged the white horizon;
in the end, fortunes road the rails west.

Black hulls with their proud nameplates embossed
in gold raced from the Banks, close-reached for home.
Salt boxes filled with *baccalao*, bartered
for rum. Men met their fate in yellow dories.
A gull's wing curved in the atomized air,
cracked hands carved a half model to cut waves,
Cape Islanders took shape from root and bole,
Men christened boats for wives and girl children.

Trawls ousted hook-and-line, filled with fish
thrown overboard, time after time. All
so some restauranteur could serve a fillet
the size of his palm, caught to order,
some stockholder could clip a coupon,
some politician could be elected,
names old as the continent disappear,
fishers, fish-cutters become eco-refugees.
Now we have remembrance, rust and rot.
Bureaucracies and empty seas are our lot.

No longer do sage cod, big as gaffers,
(Atlantic gods sporting pharaonic whiskers)
gather in our coves, waters thicken with eggs

like tapioca, beaches bear witness
to the strange lovemaking of capelin.
Seabirds drown in bilge oil, brass propellers
split open the last whales, fish spawn tumours.
We scrape the bottom for urchin, pick winkles,
dig bloodworms, strip the very rocks for weed,
in despair burn boats to the waterline.

iv. Forked Cape

The sea remembers her dead: the sea mink,
the Atlantic walrus, the Labrador duck,
the *Titanic* riven in two, her dead,
the *Bluenose* worm-eaten on a Haitian reef.
It is for us to remember the living.

It is not enough to be picturesque—
shanties bright as buoys, empty lighthouses
propped against grey rocks like theatre sets.
Not enough to fiddle like divine Celts
as we wait for the seas to fill again.

I stand at the forked Cape, named by Champlain,
bleary, watching the green sea roll away,
over the bones of the harpoon people,
            their drowned islands.
Many have stood here before me, the rocks
themselves are runes, inscribed by sou'westers,
and, some say, seafarers who tasted
wild grapes, salt-touched and tangled
            on the far shore.

Sagas lost in the landwash. The living
speak the language of the scallop and lobster,
the dialect of cod, haddock and herring,
the eloquent babble of the seabirds.

The salt, the sombre hues, the hollow sounds
mock us. I admit, a poet cannot
launch the boats, cut the bait, dry-up the nets.
All must wait for the seas to fill again.

Ova Aves

[2003]

Common Loon
Gavia immer

All bird guides begin with 'loon.'
You are most ancient, most prehistoric,

as all can attest who hear your call
oscillate across a dark lake, quirky as a quasar,

harking back to a time before humans
began to gawk at the night sky

(star-spangled like your back) and wonder,
whence all this cosmic commotion?

You are the spirit in the shaking tent,
the belief in an abiding mystery,

something alive in the mute cosmos
besides our nattering selves. A voice

that vibrates in the reptilian brain, echoing
an old word we once knew, need more than ever.

Thick-billed Murre
Uria lomvia

A ghost is clasped within your inked cameo, the blue funk
of extinction, ancestral memory of all those who came ashore,

scurvy navvy and curator alike, club in hand,
to batter the Great Auk into oblivion.

Tuxedoed and noble, you preside at the continent's edge,
rejoicing at every empty wave.

The Atlantic roils below, while your egg, clever dervish,
twirls on its precarious ledge—without a great fall.

You gargle and mumble your complaint;
your guttural chorus erects a sentinel of sound

to remind us of the cost of silence.

Ring-billed Gull
Larus delawarensis

'Land gull,' my friend says. Evolve backwards,
if you will, abandon the mothering sea,

follow in the chocolate wake of the plough,
forsaking the clean, blue line the keel makes.

Pick worms. Perhaps that is how you acquired
that indelible signature at the bill tip,

from too much probing in the black earth.
I am like that, too, carrying smudged words

at my fingertips. Loafing, waiting
for something to turn up, to swallow it whole.

Black-headed Gull
Larus ridibundus

I saw one once, tracing an arctic circle, a rarity,
another entry for the list I do not keep.

Funny thing, its head was not black at all,
but brown, which is how you know it is not

Laughing, Sabine's, nor Bonaparte's, all black-headed.
Once I hurdled the literal, I liked the irony

of describing a thing for what it is not.
For once, science takes a flier.

Look, look there! 'What?' A black-headed gull!
'Where?' See! 'Which one?' The one with the brown cap.

Killdeer
Charadrius vociferus

You might chide your mother for her seeming carelessness,
the shallow scrape where you lay. But who could gainsay her clever ploys?

She feigns this way and that, dragging her wing tip
in a sinuous line, hopscotching across the plain.

Thinking ourselves clever, we become fox,
taste the sweet flesh of this poor, earth-bound creature.

Following, we travel ever further from satisfaction.

Even you, dumb egg, play the decoy, lying
in the gravel, silent as any stone.

Soon, little one, you will put on your twin yoke
and meet the light, singing your mother's wiles.

Northern Harrier
Circus cyaneus

White, nearly round as a cue ball, your egg might
roll true on that green tableland banked behind dykes—

Tantramar, maritime prairie the sea laid down,
grain by grain, when the tide was 'asking high.'

You tilt above this reclaimed place
like a bubble in a spirit level,

tipping by degrees, as if pondering
a question of loyalty, reparation for past injustice.

You yourself suspend the laws of nature,
hanging in the sky, stalled

on upswept wings,
calling all the shots.

Red-winged Blackbird
Agelaius phoeniceus

The scarlet slash on the shoulder, bold epaulet,
reminds me of that dashing cad, Sargent Troy,

whose sabre's lethal cuts and thrusts
opened the fickle heart of Bathsheba,

Hardy's 'Queen of the Corn-Market.'
The old master preferred the commonplace,

country-born, to the flash of rank or station.
Nature, too, favors the homely,

clothing the female in a drab cloak
that hides her well among the rushes.

She is the heroine; all that matters, her fate.
The dark, flashy one may mate as he likes

or explode in a hawk's talons, his red and black
feathers cascading down like fireworks.

Emu
Dromaius novaehollandiae

So birds must fly?
To that, I, emu, put the lie.

Down under, the world on its head,
birds walk instead.

True, females lay eggs, as everywhere,
but it is the males who take care

of the clutch of seven to ten.
The striped young soon run

with their faithful parents, like dinosaurs
kicking along at 50 kilometres an hour,

in a race to outdistance time.
I, emu, am the last of my kind.

A Ship Portrait

A Novella-in-Verse

[2005]

[A conversation across time between the marine painter John O'Brien (1831-1891) and a contemporary Maritimer.]

1830s

As boys we were urchins of Water Street.
It smelt of salt cod, black rum, tar and tea.
Irishtown they called it, where my countrymen
rubbed shoulders with Negroes, clapped each other's back.
You could buy a needle or an anchor.
Without a penny, we came to learn the sails.

There seemed no end to the cut of sails
for ship, barque, brigantine, schooner, anchored
at the docks. They carried molasses and tea
from Caribe and China. On Water Street
lorries hauled it all away, while men
carted their sea-chests on their backs
            like barnacles.

Head over heel, we trundled down the steep back
of Halifax town where the ships lay at anchor,
their sails furled, linen white or brown as tea.
Up and down the shrouds and masts men
scurried, black as ants, attending to the sails
spread like a bank of cloud along Water Street.

Dodging horse and cart we crossed Water Street
to the wharves. Masts and spars crossed, tees
towering above us, rocking back
and forth as the great ships lay at anchor.
Mizzen, top gallant, royal, jib, all sails
we dreamt of working when we were men.

To us, sailors were the only true men.
We scorned all others behind their backs.
Not for us to trudge up whale-back streets,
to sit in parlours, shore-bound, sipping tea.
We wanted to feel the wind in our sails,
slip into far away ports to drop anchor.

It was to the sea we looked to anchor
our dreams— sea-bound, we would never look back.
Water would divide us from lesser men
when we climbed aloft to unfurl the sails.
Poor lads would hail us from Water Street,
the words grow fainter: *Oil Clothes, Dry Goods, Tea* ...

stencilled on the chandleries. The teeming
ocean would beckon, the trades fill our sails—
not knowing if one day they would blow us back.

We still have our Water Streets
with their harping gulls, their raw smells,
but the ships are long gone.
Only the hulls of derelict draggers
litter the shore.
Wharves teeter on rotten piles
where the tall ships once berthed.
We need you, O'Brien, to bring them back,
ballasted with the exotic —

ivory backscratcher,

        Shanghai,

peacock quill cigar case,

        Java,

four whales teeth,

        Indian Ocean,

wild boar tusks,

        New Zealand,

maté cup and bombilla,

        Buenos Aires,

opium pipe,

        China,

ant egg necklace,

        Cape Town,

pearl fish hook,

        Solomon Islands,

war club,

        Australia —

preserved under glass
like your portraits, O'Brien,
testament to our great wanderings.

Once we were cosmopolitan,
once we set our hopes like our sails,
seaward, to all points of the compass.

Once we were at home in Bombay
or Rangoon,
familiar in Melbourne
or Hong Kong,
masters wherever
our keels
cut water.

1840s

My father was an Artist in Hair,
procured the finest locks from New York.
The ladies piled them high, fake cumuli
propped on their porcelain brows.
High society donned the pawned tresses
of the poor, already bought and paid for –
even the hairs of their lousy heads.
I would wig the sky with clouds instead,
cirri, the portent of a storm worrying
        the clear blue.
Sails, you might say, were the gowns
swathing my wooden ladies of the waves.
Next to the mute, coiffed mannequins
I propped my first portraits, as did Turner,
his father like my own, a Barber.
The Dutchman, van de Velde the Younger,
hurt us both to paint–his storms at sea
wigged with white caps pulled us under.

Boys of good character, O'Brien,
at first we hardly knew
what was happening
as we felt the first tug,
the undertow carrying us
into deeper water.

Yacht Race, 1850

The officers got up a regatta.
Already my sketch of the flagship
and squadron southbound for Bermuda
had been celebrated in the *Nova Scotian* —
I was not yet nineteen. The clouds cleared
while the wind, N. N. W. off the land, filled
the sails but hardly rippled the harbour.
Half the town, decked out in holiday colours,
gathered at the dock. The rum and bets went down.
The *Pyramus*—Nelson's proud booty—flew
a pyramid of flags, gunnel to topmast.

Sloops, schooners, cutters and yawls tacked
about the old lady like sea-dancers
coupled in feverish reel or quadrille.
I kept watch to freeze this motion:
            in the fifth race
I saw what I was looking for—*Mystery,*
Eclipse, Wanderer, close-hauled on the port tack.
Looking back, these three might have been my fates.
.
That day I attended to the sea, set of sail,
sky and its gathering fleet of torn clouds.
What is a ship without the sky's weather?
(Even Ruskin knew that, Turner too.)
The canvas is a mirror for cloud-light.
"The rain cloud," Ruskin said, "carries its own wind.
It reveals all that it is beautiful,
conceals all that is hurtful, makes the paltry
look vast, the ponderous, light and airy."

Skipper balanced on her bow, *Mystery*
tacked into the sky's dark embrace,
a foreboding my eye could not ignore.

                                        Mystery heeled over,
the ivory spray scrimshawed her black hull.
Her pursuers fell off the right margin
        of my canvas.
Everything rushed away, soundless,
while the picture composed itself

— "a very clever specimen," they said.

Who knows what posterity will preserve —
something we pray? Perhaps it is not
all for naught.

Halifax Harbour, Sunset, 1853

What was it I wanted to paint, you ask —
the sea (though it is only a harbour view),
the sky with its October colours,
the town encrusting the fort-crowned hill,
the ships loitering on the waves
as the sun sinks down, or the sailor
with the pike pole spearing a deadhead
as if it were a shark?—I can't remember.
The harbour was my ready canvas
      —Bedford to Sambro—
stretched daily before my eyes,
a pageant of iron, sailcloth, wood.
I plodded the planks, itinerant,
in search of a commission, patron's
largesse. Most days there was none.
Why not, then, paint the scene itself—
the nautical panorama unrolling
      like a travelling sideshow.

Foreground: the sea begins in shadow,
in depth, roiled and discontent.
The ships, frigate and merchant brig,
stand guard on either side of the canvas
      —Charybdis and Scylla—
on one side, war, on the other, commerce,
aspects of the same thing, if you ask me.
The setting sun floods city and basin,
a steamer scrawls its inky statement,
schooners tack to starboard or to port
(their sails catch the light as sharply as the wind),
the sun gilds the dome of St. George's,
as if this were Byzantium.
But it was the sky that spoke urgently—
I remember now—its last light

rising to meet the azure of descending night.
("The sky," Ruskin said, "does not remain
the same for two inches together.")
Lemon into peach, ochre into vermillion,
       vermillion into ultramarine.

Look now, O'Brien,
what is familiar
in the harbour
you knew so well,
besides the corrugations
(lamp black, cobalt, purple madder)
the long susurrus of the sea,
painted with quick flicks
of the wrist, white pigment
flying from wave crests; besides
predictable gulls and cormorants,
port mascots riding the chop,
the terraced hump of George's
(abandoned but still beaconed) stepping
tentatively into the deep;
and beyond, where the sky's greyness
blends with water,
the lighthouse on Devil's Island
barely keeping its head up,
like a drowning man?
These everyday vistas
as common for you
as for us.

But look here, O'Brien:
instead of unseeable wind, the flare,
effluvia, the slick of oil in air and water.
Oil rigs jacked
above the waves
like daddy-long-legs,

drilling the sands
where so many of your ships
foundered.
Steel instead of wood: two spans
suspended in fog
in the morning,
in the afternoon
touching both shores,
the selvages of your world.
Instead of clippers
dressed in tiers of canvas,
like floating wedding cakes,
container ships, ungraceful bulks
with boxes as big as railcars,
piled impossibly high—

not a sail in sight, O'Brien.

An alien scene but for the ultramarines,
        the soul of water,
and crazy Ruskin's vaulted skies.

Portrait of a Ship, 1855

Now I began to knock them off, one
every week or so. I always gave them
what they wanted —"under full sail"—
as if I were painting their own portraits.
How do men become wood, iron, hemp
       and canvas?
Or is it the wind, waves and scudding skies
we wear in our guts, on our faces?
We are all prone to becoming what we make,
captive to our own manic compass.

Show them in the harbour, landfall or departure,
either way within sight of land—lighthouse,
headland or island to port or starboard.
Show them the certainty of payoff,
the promise of good passage:
the pilot ship close by, the burden
       of navigation lifted.

       The ships grow and grow,
no longer infinitesimal specks,
mere pencil crosses on the flat ocean
       of the tract chart.
They fly their house flags like badges of courage;
they are not yet lost, condemned, broken up,
       cut-down or sold.
In my art they would always be whole;
for this flattery they paid me.
In my art, the winds were always propitious,
the way clear, the owners' fortune assured.
The portrait granted them what fate withholds.

Look closely at these pictures of perfection —
you may see the vanity of commerce,

but always the sky is making weather,
the sea's cruel undercurrent is pulling
the enterprise toward the patient rocks.
The violet in the clouds, each wavelet,
conjures doubt, foreshadowing disaster.

You gave them what they wanted, O'Brien,
who could blame you for that? After all
you had a living to make. You gave us
what we now need, not just the faithful record
of the ships (their cut and rig),
but an image of a better time, outward-
looking, not close-hauled against the shore,
    insular.

Still we sit in judgement, spew epithets—
"primitive, hack, potboiler, provincial, naive"—
as if we did not see ourselves better
after you had portrayed us as stately ships.
In the end, when the brokers' fortunes
are spent, the heroics of iron men acted out,
what is left but your art?

11 November 1857

Dear Father:-

My master, J. W. Carmichael, Esq.,
is not long back from the Baltic Campaign.
His work in the *Illustrated London News*
was known to me. All said I could not find
a better teacher. In my first work he found
little to correct—why then had I come?
"The fresh sea, mid-day, with a blue streak
        in the sky"
is his credo. "Give them what they see,
or want to see," he says, "then they will buy."

You can see there was little to learn
in England—that is, until I saw Turner:
The Shipwreck and *Dutch Boats in a Gale.*
Carmichael's seas are a grand monotony,
while Turner's are "a dizzy whirl of rushing,
writhing, tortured rage," as Ruskin says,
"an anarchy of enormous power."
The sky is roiling soot as if all the chimneys
of London belched their brimstone smoke at once.
The northern seas are crushed beneath this weather,
men, women and boats mere flotsam.
The rescue boat circles the maelstrom;
behind looms the dismasted wreck.
It is impossible to know whether
the world is being drowned or resurrected.
Avalanche, deluge, shipwreck and fire —
as Hazlitt said, "They are pictures of nothing."

Upon first seeing Turner—vertigo!
Did you feel yourself go under, O'Brien,
a drowning man sucking his last innocent breath?

Broken Vessel

Thirty-Five Days in the Desert

[2007]

6.

Crossers of the Sands,
look to the night,
the quarter moon
and its companion star
shining in the black chart
of the desert sky.
Then, take direction.

7.

The desert is a sea
(as everyone knows),
the migrating sun
glancing off
endless crests.
Cast out
among whale-back dunes,
you may drift for days or weeks
in search of those green islands
of the blest—
and die of thirst,
like the sailor
maddened by the sight
of water all around.

9.

In the desert
we see water

everywhere, dig
and dig

until the well
fills

with water,
or despair.

12.

Atop the *yardang*,
spear in hand,

the soldier keeps watch
over the valley

for the enemy
who never comes.

To pass time

he carves his hand,
his foot, in the rock,

signatures;

the birds and animals
he has killed;

V's for the women
he wishes to love;

the unbearably long
days of his duty.

13.

Does it matter
if Cleopatra clasped
the asp or asps
to one or two
of her golden breasts—

those orbs that inspired
treachery, knives
in the back, tectonic
acts that shook
far away Rome?

One asp, two asps,
does it matter?

One bite, the *omal* say,
there is only time
to smoke one cigarette.

Empires fall.
Does it matter if one's death
is imperial or common?

23.

The hawk has chosen for his perch
the wreckage of a ruined church
nearly as old as the Apostles.
He cares not for the idea of a single god,
unless that god is a hawk
silhouetted against
the life-giving sun.

29.

Rain returns
us to our senses—

the smell of wet earth,
the taste of wet skin,

antidote to the dry
dissertations

of the desert, beating
down upon our brows,

year upon year,
without answer.

31.

What can be said
about the silence
of the desert
that does not sound
like the decrepit patter
of broken pots
underfoot?

32.

On the Long Road
camel bones bleach

in the sun, bitter
reminders of the desert way—

the ceaseless journeying. Better
to die here than make the long climb

from the desert floor. At the plateau
to find more desert stretching forth

like the forty days
fallen behind.

35·

We need things
that cannot be found.

If they do not exist,
all the better—

Zerzura, the Lost Oasis
of the Little Birds,

calling to us sweetly
as the desert lark.

New Poems

The Tubercular Calf

The great golden cows angled queenly
through the summer grasses, their bellies
high as my tow head, me proud
to be learning the yeoman's language—
Cow boss, come boss, come home, Bossie—
and them, horned goddesses, parading up
the retaining wall to the milking parlour,
casting their sidelong hermetic blessings
      as they passed.
This, I thought, was my inheritance:
red and barred hens, many teated sows,
      queenly cows.

But then the sickly calves began to come,
one after another like a biblical plague,
wobbly-legged, streaked with mustard feces—
      dead within days.
I ministered to them with my mother,
bottle nursing their slick muzzles, eager
tongues, like them not knowing this was the end.
Soon the barns would echo empty,
the ghostly cattle would come no longer
      when called—
Cow boss, come boss, come home, Bossie—
I would have to learn a new language,
find meaning among animals of my own kind.

Returning

All my life I have been returning there,
in dreams to that first place—home,
a farmhouse on a hill above a river,
above the attic, to a secret room—in the air?

I first went there out of loneliness
(even then it seems), a room filled with children,
like me seeking solace. An old woman
dressed in black, like Whistler's mother, watched over us.

In the old house was such a place, a crawl space
behind the book case where one could hide,
look out through the books, spy on the living,
what a writer does from the beginning.

The house, the one in dreams, is never the same.
Sometimes it is abandoned, a disaster;
I pick my way through crumbling lathe and plaster,
up decrepit back stairs, seeking the upper room.

There is no getting there from here. If there were,
what would I find—the children grown old,
the old woman in black gone, my way barred?
All my life I will be returning, but where?

Geography: On First Discovering Elizabeth Bishop in a Used Bookstore in Manhattan

for Sandra Barry

Geography III
(so plain but for the oddity
of Roman numerals),
I lift it down and begin,
by chance, "From narrow provinces..."
and suddenly am riding beside her,
in that beat-up bus of blue enamel,
Acadian Lines along my home shore,
past the unspeakably quiet
clapboard houses, barnacle
white churches, through
all the Economies, over
the mountain, where bracketed
between Capes Split and Sharp
the Five Islands rise
from lavender flats—
Moose, Diamond, Long, Egg and Pinnacle—
thinking to myself,
I can navigate this poem
with my eyes closed:
you are one of ours come home.

Miss Bishop, you have returned
to find the school, "high, bare and white clapboarded,"
still there, and that "echo of a scream"
hanging forever where you left it,
above the iron bridge
in the nameless "Village."
This was the place, as you said,

"of fish and bread and tea,"
of fish houses and first deaths.

Thinking to myself,
you could be any one of us—
my mother (also Elizabeth)
whose father was drowned in winter seas,
whose mother, like yours,
was made mad by sudden loss.
Like you, "a country mouse,"
my mother went to a better house,
to learn what "a girl should know,"
not what she needed, not love, no.

Odd attraction: we must return
to this pinched peninsula,
this "narrow province"
with its Roman name,
wherever we may go—New York or Rio.
If born here, you can hardly get away;
if not, you are always come-from-away.
You are from "up-shore" or "down-shore",
          this our crazy compass.
It seems we leave only to return,
like your obsessed sandpiper, looking,
looking, for what the "long tides" bring home.

Summer Morning, Reading
James Wright's Poems

I have wasted my life
—James Wright

The read pages of poetry curl up
in the dampness of July
like leaves where aphids have fed.

These days so like the fogbound
mornings of childhood,
so green, so ready to begin—

to let the sun shine in.

These the measures of our days:
the read and the unread,
the living and the dead—

the said and the unsaid.

This one morning
like no other, or one
half remembered,

days divided by the crows' cawing,
the little birds perched outside
our windows commencing to sing.

Rembrandt Laughing

Masters laugh—
greatness can be a belly laugh
erupting through a square, almost brutish
face, crowned by a foppish hat.
Rascal, the laugh curling into fullness
at the corner of the ale-besotted mouth,
an oblique emotion, ironic,
off-colour as a W.C. Field joke.
Yet, as Freud said,
so much darkness, so little light:
look at the saint cross-hatched
in the glowering twilight of good and evil,
or the lovers fornicating in the deep grasses,
under an all-seeing, unforgiving sky.
But again and again, he etched
his own face, eighty five times
to be exact. Looking into a copper plate,
he laughed at the spectacle of himself—
an old reprobate bearing
a master's satisfied smile,
human as Christ on the Cross,
a pratfalling vaudevillian.

Four Ages

1. Bone

Helmeted men masked behind tinted glass
menace the footpaths, leave behind reptilian tracks,

or four-wheeling, rut the snow
like a moose in heat,

while I, balanced on two wooden slabs,
must step aside, am left behind,

like a primitive in the headlong
whoosh of time—like the deer herders

strapping on the long bones of horses
to skate across the frozen land.

II. Fire

The earth is surfacing, bloated,
floating up like a drowned animal,
its tawny fur matted, dirty with itself.

April light is like iodine dropped
into the eye, darkness opening
to swallow its psychedelic burnishings.

Men are burning the old year, shovel,
wet burlap in hand to watch over
hot window panes, as if they could see
    into Hades.

What do they desire?—To bring forth
the first green shoots, risen from the earth
like an albino girl with flowers
in her unworldly white arms.

III. Brass

In fields are fat, plastic-wrapped marshmallows,
by-gone are the bristling rectangular bales.

One summer I hefted ten-thousand, three times:
field to hayrack, hayrack to barn, third time

high up in the mow to the roof's airless peak
where swallows came and went. Honey twine

rope-burned furrows in my fingers,
stubble needled my arms, my back

grew strong. At day's end we doused
ourselves like tempered iron in the water trough.

Seeing the new mown fields, I remember,
for a season I was brazen, hard as Hector.

iv. Silver

Mackinawed men onion-bag crab apples
to lure white-tailed deer between their cross hairs.

Men fork eelgrass into truck beds this time of year,
pile it high against sills to thwart winter drafts,

each act a shoring up against leanness,
a staving off of the coming cold.

Even the leaves are melodramatic
in their flaring, dizzy falling to earth;

even I am a figure in this seasonal tableau:
plot to anchor iron in the jawbone of a fish,

only to release her, silvery, egg-laden,
to feed upon herself six months under ice.

Going to the Woods Alone

I blue the fresh fallen snow.
Above a jet scribes winter sky—white lines
of breath mimicking my twin tracks.
I push up the hill opening into pasture,
where the sun is impaled on a portcullis
of black spruce, past the open field
tattooed with the dying stalks of rhodora,
brown as dried blood, follow along
in the tree harvester's ruts, into the woods
where a silence descends. Here are other tracks—
a coyote circling through the cutting, hungry, disconsolate.

It is late, the moon high, the setting sun
streaks of disembodied light. Time to return
to the kitchen, to the study, to await
my wife's homecoming. More time to be alone
with my murmuring heart trailing along behind.
The next day, I learn my seventy-year-old neighbour
chainsawed a sixty-foot spruce—
its rotten heartwood splitting—
cracking his jaw in three places
when it fell the wrong way,
kicked back like a workhorse.
He drove the tractor through the darkening woods,
bloodied, staying conscious long enough to get home.
Neighbours agree: no man should go to the woods alone.

A Poem in Praise of the Poet's Wife

for Catherine

You reach behind to unhook
your brassiere and the angle

of your arms makes wings.
Below you are bare—

I should like to silkscreen
the carnal cross down there

as you bend over our bed,
to work out the physics

of bodies that attract.
Space curves, satellites sling shot

past the planets on their dark
journeys to the stars.

Before the lights go out,
or in the morning light

you stand naked, still a little wet
from the shower. I have seen

this so often before,
it should not matter,

but it does, it does.
For the moment

I am distracted
by the act, the unloosening,

the slipping free: doublet graces.
Turn, let me hold them

instead—in my eye, in my palms,
in my cupping mouth.

Let me fill my silence
with something other

than words. It is
winter out there.

Bifocals

It can take two lives to make one—
the unfulfilled father, the fortunate son.

I see the world with two sets of eyes,
like you looking up from the pages,

peering, owl-like, over bifocals.
Like you I see reality doubled:

out of focus, too near, the far world
made clear through the lens of words.

My Father on the Church Roof

My father is up there, on his knees,
on the church roof where he shouldn't be,
clinging at a mortal angle
to the coves and gables,
a mere man balanced
between belief and faith.

My father is up there, on his knees,
on the church roof, buttressed in air.
Will he fall, I pray not;
if so, will he be saved, I pray—
the questions we ask ourselves,
and god, if we believe?

My father is up there, on his knees,
on the church roof, halfway to heaven,
trying to keep bread on the table,
rain from falling on the bowed heads
of the faithful, to keep from falling
himself, into eternity.

My father is up there, on his knees,
on the church roof, over fifty,
still unsure whether he believes
in anything more than he can measure,
cut and fit—in the shadow of the exalted steeple,
the salt horizon straight as a T-square.

Signal EDITIONS

Carmine Starnino, Editor
Michael Harris, Founding Editor

SELECTED POEMS David Solway
THE MULBERRY MEN David Solway
A SLOW LIGHT Ross Leckie
NIGHT LETTERS Bill Furey
COMPLICITY Susan Glickman
A NUN'S DIARY Ann Diamond
CAVALIER IN A ROUNDHEAD SCHOOL Errol MacDonald
VEILED COUNTRIES/LIVES Marie-Claire Blais (Translated by Michael Harris)
BLIND PAINTING Robert Melançon (Translated by Philip Stratford)
SMALL HORSES & INTIMATE BEASTS Michel Garneau
   (Translated by Robert McGee)
IN TRANSIT Michael Harris
THE FABULOUS DISGUISE OF OURSELVES Jan Conn
ASHBOURN John Reibetanz
THE POWER TO MOVE Susan Glickman
MAGELLAN'S CLOUDS Robert Allen
MODERN MARRIAGE David Solway
K. IN LOVE Don Coles
THE INVISIBLE MOON Carla Hartsfield
ALONG THE ROAD FROM EDEN George Ellenbogen
DUNINO Stephen Scobie
KINETIC MUSTACHE Arthur Clark
RUE SAINTE FAMILLE Charlotte Hussey
HENRY MOORE'S SHEEP Susan Glickman
SOUTH OF THE TUDO BEM CAFÉ Jan Conn
THE INVENTION OF HONEY Ricardo Sternberg
EVENINGS AT LOOSE ENDS Gérald Godin (Translated by Judith Cowan)
THE PROVING GROUNDS Rhea Tregebov
LITTLE BIRD Don Coles
HOMETOWN Laura Lush
FORTRESS OF CHAIRS Elisabeth Harvor
NEW & SELECTED POEMS Michael Harris
BEDROCK David Solway
TERRORIST LETTERS Ann Diamond
THE SIGNAL ANTHOLOGY Edited by Michael Harris
MURMUR OF THE STARS: SELECTED SHORTER POEMS Peter Dale Scott
WHAT DANTE DID WITH LOSS Jan Conn
MORNING WATCH John Reibetanz
JOY IS NOT MY PROFESSION Muhammad al-Maghut
   (Translated by John Asfour and Alison Burch)
WRESTLING WITH ANGELS: SELECTED POEMS Doug Beardsley
HIDE & SEEK Susan Glickman
MAPPING THE CHAOS Rhea Tregebov
FIRE NEVER SLEEPS Carla Hartsfield

THE RHINO GATE POEMS George Ellenbogen
SHADOW CABINET Richard Sanger
MAP OF DREAMS Ricardo Sternberg
THE NEW WORLD Carmine Starnino
THE LONG COLD GREEN EVENINGS OF SPRING Elisabeth Harvor
FAULT LINE Laura Lush
WHITE STONE: THE ALICE POEMS Stephanie Bolster
KEEP IT ALL Yves Boisvert (Translated by Judith Cowan)
THE GREEN ALEMBIC Louise Fabiani
THE ISLAND IN WINTER Terence Young
A TINKERS' PICNIC Peter Richardson
SARACEN ISLAND: THE POEMS OF ANDREAS KARAVIS David Solway
BEAUTIES ON MAD RIVER: SELECTED AND NEW POEMS Jan Conn
WIND AND ROOT Brent MacLaine
HISTORIES Andrew Steinmetz
ARABY Eric Ormsby
WORDS THAT WALK IN THE NIGHT Pierre Morency
    (Translated by Lissa Cowan and René Brisebois)
A PICNIC ON ICE: SELECTED POEMS Matthew Sweeney
HELIX: NEW AND SELECTED POEMS John Steffler
HERESIES: THE COMPLETE POEMS OF ANNE WILKINSON, 1924-1961
    Edited by Dean Irvine
CALLING HOME Richard Sanger
FIELDER'S CHOICE Elise Partridge
MERRYBEGOT Mary Dalton
MOUNTAIN TEA Peter Van Toorn
AN ABC OF BELLY WORK Peter Richardson
RUNNING IN PROSPECT CEMETERY Susan Glickman
MIRABEL Pierre Nepveu (Translated by Judith Cowan)
POSTSCRIPT Geoffrey Cook
STANDING WAVE Robert Allen
THERE, THERE Patrick Warner
HOW WE ALL SWIFTLY: THE FIRST SIX BOOKS Don Coles
THE NEW CANON: AN ANTHOLOGY OF CANADIAN POETRY
    Edited by Carmine Starnino
OUT TO DRY IN CAPE BRETON Anita Lahey
RED LEDGER Mary Dalton
REACHING FOR CLEAR David Solway
OX Christopher Patton
THE MECHANICAL BIRD Asa Boxer
SYMPATHY FOR THE COURIERS Peter Richardson
MORNING GOTHIC: NEW AND SELECTED POEMS George Ellenbogen
36 CORNELIAN AVENUE Christopher Wiseman
THE EMPIRE'S MISSING LINKS Walid Bitar
PENNY DREADFUL Shannon Stewart
THE STREAM EXPOSED WITH ALL ITS STONES D.G. Jones
PURE PRODUCT Jason Guriel
ANIMALS OF MY OWN KIND Harry Thurston

 Véhicule Press